Original title:
Snickers in the Sycamores

Copyright © 2025 Creative Arts Management OÜ
All rights reserved.

Author: William Hawthorne
ISBN HARDBACK: 978-1-80567-328-6
ISBN PAPERBACK: 978-1-80567-627-0

Whispers Among the Branches

In the trees, giggles rise,
Squirrels plotting, oh what lies!
Acorns dropped with cheeky flair,
Forest secrets float in air.

Laughter spills from every nook,
Mischief hides in every crook.
Leaves are rustling, stories spun,
Nature's jest has just begun.

Laughter Beneath the Canopy

Shade above, a playful crowd,
Nature's chorus, lively, loud.
In the glen, grasses sway,
Bouncing jokes in light of day.

Chirps and hoots, a funny show,
Silly antics all aglow.
Timers tick with joking squeeze,
Whimsical fun on the breeze.

Secrets of the Sylvan Grove

In the grove, whispers weave,
Tales of pranks the trees believe.
Barking dogs, a snicker spree,
Nature laughs so heartily!

Branches dance with joyful clinks,
Mischief glossed in playful winks.
Hiding spots with laughter flare,
All around, a jolly air.

Joyful Echoes in the Leaves

As sunlight threads through green delight,
Jokes are shared both day and night.
Each rustle sings of silly fun,
Underneath the sky so blue.

A gust of wind plays tag with sound,
Joyful echoes all around.
Leaves chuckle as they drift and play,
In the grove, we laugh away.

Breezy Bliss Under the Branches

Laughter swirls, breezes play,
Squirrels dance in a witty display.
Leaves chuckle as they spin around,
Joyful giggles rise from the ground.

Birds gossip with a chirpy cheer,
Their silly tunes bring the heart near.
A playful breeze tickles the face,
Nature joins in this merry race.

Merriment in the Mist

In the fog, where shadows creep,
Mischievous whispers make us leap.
The trees share secrets, soft and light,
In a joyful jig, they sway in delight.

Misty giggles float through the air,
As creatures gather without a care.
Laughter echoes, a playful tune,
Under the watch of a chuckling moon.

Lighthearted Lullabies

The winds sing songs, oh so sweet,
Tickling the toes of your happy feet.
Branches sway, with laughter they tease,
Spreading joy through the rustling leaves.

Crickets chirp in a rhythmic beat,
In the twilight, where day and night meet.
Bouncing shadows dance with glee,
Cuddled in laughter, wild and free.

Cheering the Trees

Under broad canopies, glee ignites,
Joyful rustlings on starry nights.
Branches sway in a fun parade,
Leaves clap hands, never dismayed.

Chirps and caws in playful trends,
Nature's orchestra never ends.
With every rustle, laughter flows,
In this haven, humor grows.

Twinkling Chuckles Among the Branches

In the shade where shadows play,
Squirrels giggle night and day.
Beneath the boughs where critters thrive,
Peculiar laughter comes alive.

A tiny bird with quite a flair,
Dances 'round without a care.
Branches sway with each delight,
As munching squirrels steal the night.

Raccoons prance and clap their paws,
While mischief reigns without a cause.
Acorns tumble, chaos reigns,
Joy spills out like summer rains.

Underneath the moonlit glow,
Chortles rise while breezes blow.
Nature's jesters take the stage,
In this forest, fun's the gauge.

Lightheartedness of the Leafy Lull

In the grove where laugh tracks play,
Green canopies burst with joy each day.
Nuts roll down like chuckling men,
Laughter rings from tree to glen.

A beaming frog croaks a tune,
Berry breezes stir and swoon.
Leaves flutter like giggling friends,
Tickling humor never ends.

Whimsical winds tease the trees,
As playful whispers float with ease.
Underneath the towering green,
Every creature's mischief seen.

With every rustle, jest appears,
The softest chuckles drown our fears.
Together in this leafy space,
Laughter thrives, a warm embrace.

Mischief in the Meadow

Squirrels giggle, tails a-twirl,
Grasshoppers leap, giving a whirl.
Flowers chat in colors so bright,
While bees buzz tales, a pure delight.

Bouncing balls of fluff in the air,
A game of hide and seek, beware!
Laughter echoes, the sun shines wide,
As critters play, with joy, they glide.

Chuckles Among the Bark

Tree trunks whisper, tongue-in-cheek,
Branches sway as if to peek.
A raccoon prances on a spree,
Joking with the buzzing bee.

The owl hoots with a sly surprise,
While beetles march, oh how they rise!
Their tiny dance, a funny sight,
Among the leaves, they twist in flight.

Smiles in the Sunlight

Sunbeams tickle, warm the ground,
Joyful laughter all around.
Worms wriggle, with a wiggle and shake,
As daisies sway, in giggles they wake.

A playful breeze makes leaves dart,
Nature's jesters play their part.
The skies beam down, a golden thread,
Bringing forth smiles where laughter's bred.

Delight Under the Canopy

Shade and laughter overlap,
A picnic spread, oh what a flap!
Chirping crickets take the stage,
In the leafy world, we turn the page.

Frogs croak jokes that leave us in fits,
While dandelions share their wits.
Under the canopy, life is bold,
In this realm, the laughter unfolds.

Joyful Murmurs of Nature

Beneath the boughs, the squirrels play,
Chasing shadows throughout the day.
With acorns tossed and laughter loud,
They jest among the leafy crowd.

A bird hops close, its song a cheer,
Echoing soft, for all to hear.
The breeze joins in, a chuckling tease,
Whispering secrets through the trees.

Treetop Tease

From lofty heights, a cheeky twig,
Swings and sways, not very big.
It pokes at branches, then you'll see,
A sassy leaf, quite boldly free.

With every rustle, giggles flare,
A dance of green, up in the air.
The sun peeks in, with gleeful grins,
"Mischief's alive," the tree trunk sins.

Lighthearted in the Grove

A bunny hops, its ears a-flop,
In this lighthearted, leafy shop.
It shares a wink, a silly show,
While flowers nod and giggle low.

A friendly ant, with tiny might,
Marches on, in sheer delight.
He points to clouds, so fluffy white,
"Look up, my friends, it's quite a sight!"

Mirth in the Meadow

In fields of gold, a weasel darts,
Playing tricks, with nimble arts.
It stumbles through the patchy grass,
With every leap, it seems to laugh.

The daisies dance, bright heads in tow,
Joining in on the goofy show.
Butterflies flit, in colors bold,
Spreading joy, a sight to behold.

Radiant Revelations Under the Canopy

Beneath the branches wide and deep,
A giggle bounces, making us peep.
Sneaky squirrels in a playful race,
Chewing on nuts with a grin on their face.

The sunlight dances through leaves up high,
As we uncover laughter that won't run dry.
Whispers of mischief in the warm breeze,
Nature's own jester, putting minds at ease.

Smirking Shadows Beneath the Sun

Shadows stretch with a cheeky grin,
While laughter erupts beneath the skin.
A picnic blanket sprawls on the ground,
With surprises hidden waiting to be found.

The ants march on with a silly parade,
Little comedians, never afraid.
We chuckle and snicker, 'What a delight!'
In this warm moment, everything feels right.

Daydreams of Delight in the Drive

As we cruise along with spirits high,
Bouncing in rhythm, oh my, oh my!
Windows down, we sing loud and proud,
In this merry car, we're a jovial crowd.

The mystery bag holds candy galore,
Every new treat opens joy's door.
With sticky fingers and smiles so wide,
Adventure awaits on this wild ride.

Roots of Revelry

At the base of a tree where dreams collide,
Laughter spills out, we can't hide.
The roots come alive, as they twist and weave,
Tales of joy that we all believe.

Jumping around with a jubilant cheer,
Echoes of fun that we hold dear.
Sun-kissed moments that twinkle and glow,
In the heart of nature, our merriment flows.

Echoing Giggles through the Glades

In the glades where the shadows play,
 Lively whispers dance and sway.
A squirrel ambushes with a nut,
 Laughter erupts, oh what a cut!

A rabbit hops with glee so spry,
 Trying to leap, oh my, oh my!
The leaves chuckle as they take flight,
 Sprightly mischief, hearts feel light.

With each step, a soft crunch sings,
 Carried forth on mischievous wings.
The brook chuckles with every splash,
 Funny faces in the wild dash!

Through the trees, a chorus rings,
 Nature's laughter freely springs.
Underneath the vast blue skies,
 Giggles echo, oh, what a surprise!

Playful Whispers of the Woods

In the woods, the secrets leap,
Where shadows play and joy runs deep.
A fox curtsies, tosses a wink,
Off he bounds, don't stop to think.

The owls hoot in comical tones,
Echoes of laughter from their stones.
A raccoon prances with a pie,
"What's for dessert?" he's slyly spry!

Hidden paths hold jokes untold,
With every step, a story bold.
The breeze tickles through the trees,
Nature's humor brings us to our knees.

With winks and giggles in each flow,
The woods' whimsical ways do glow.
In playful whispers, joy's unfurled,
A funny magic in the world!

Serene Chuckles In the Shade

Beneath the trees, the sunlight plays,
In quiet nooks where laughter stays.
Butterflies dance with joyful glee,
Serene chuckles from you and me.

A clever crow with shiny tricks,
Perches high, and swiftly flicks.
A tumbleweed rolls with surprise,
Chasing shadows, no need to disguise.

While daisies nod in sweet delight,
Each petal sways, feeling quite right.
A breeze that tickles, soft and light,
Whispers secrets, oh what a sight!

In shade we find our playful heart,
Where nature's humor plays its part.
With each chuckle, life's serenade,
In peaceful bliss, we laugh, we wade.

Warmth in the Woodland

In woodland realms where sunlight beams,
Laughter spills and wildness dreams.
A chubby bear in plaid attire,
Dancing round with pure desire!

The trees sway gently, sharing jokes,
As giddy critters play like folks.
A chipmunk scatters nuts in haste,
Creating chaos, full of taste.

Patches of sunlight warm the ground,
With giggles echoing all around.
A squirrel slips, lands with a thud,
Rolling leafy laughter, what a flood!

Through the woods, we find our cheer,
With every stumble, love draws near.
In warmth of nature, we collide,
With giggles bursting, side by side!

Elation Under the Emerald Arch

In the shade where the green leaves play,
   Squirrels dance in a silly ballet.
  Chasing shadows, hopping around,
   Laughter echoes, a joyful sound.

  Beneath the arch where secrets lie,
  Chipmunks giggle as they pass by.
   Each rustle, a cue for a prank,
  Nature's jesters, no formality rank.

 A picnic turned playful in the glade,
   Sandwiches fly, a food parade.
  Lemonade spills, a fizzy spree,
   What a sight, oh, look and see!

With roots entwined, they share the thrill,
  Joyful whispers, each heart to fill.
  Under emerald branches, we unite,
  In laughter's embrace, all feels right.

Jests in the Juniper Dreams

In the junipers where dreams collide,
Breezes chuckle, with joy the tide.
A butterfly slips, an unexpected flight,
Landing on noses, what a funny sight!

The rabbits gather, planning a jest,
Witty banter in their cozy nest.
Whispers of mischief mixed with cheer,
Juniper's laughter blooms near and dear.

A shadow leaps, it's a prancing goat,
With a wink and a hop, it floats like a boat.
In that moment, the world seems bright,
Nature's theater, pure delight.

Under the gaze of stars so bold,
Humor and mischief together unfold.
In the juniper's embrace, we frolic and play,
Creating memories that forever will stay.

Whispers Beneath the Leaves

Beneath the canopy where shadows blend,
Whispers fly, on them we depend.
A crow caws jokes, perched high with glee,
Tickles the heart, sets spirits free.

Dancing ants march to a rhythm divine,
In their tiny world, everything's fine.
A pizzicato of giggles underfoot,
Where silly chaos finds its root.

A feather drifts from a passing bird,
Landing softly, not a sound heard.
Giggles erupt from a hidden nook,
Nature's comedy, an open book.

From leaf to leaf, giggling sways,
Swaying in rhythm, in joyous arrays.
Amid rustling whispers, laughter's decree,
Life's humor blooms, wild and free.

Laughter in the Limbs

Amongst the limbs where the creatures play,
Laughter rings out through the green ballet.
A raccoon rolls, all fluff and cheer,
Belly up, without any fear.

The branches bounce with a giggle or two,
As a bushy-tailed friend swoops through.
Sprinkling chuckles like petals in spring,
Joyous sounds of nature take wing.

A hidden nook, a surprise awaits,
Marshmallows fall, oh, what fun it creates!
S'mores and smiles, under starlit skies,
Together we cherish, life's sweet surprise.

High in the air where the breezes sway,
Laughter finds us, come what may.
In the arms of the trees, we swing and twirl,
In a world of humor, come join the whirl!

Gleeful Secrets of Ancient Woods

In the rustling leaves, secrets hide,
Laughter bubbles like a bubbling tide.
Squirrels dance near the knotted trees,
Sharing jokes with the buzzing bees.

Fungi giggle in pastel hues,
While shadows drape in silly views.
A fox with a hat and a cheeky grin,
Whispers tales of cheeky sin.

Branches sway to a laughter tune,
Tickling the air beneath the moon.
Mushrooms whisper to the wise old owl,
As the crickets join with a giddy growl.

In these woods, mischief reigns supreme,
Sprightly antics, a woodland dream.
Echoes of giggles, so pure and bright,
Craft a world of delight tonight.

Whimsy in the Woodland Whisper

Through the thicket, whispers glide,
Tales of mischief that can't abide.
Bunnies in bowties chase their tails,
While clever crows play tricks with snails.

The brook sings, a comical tune,
Dancing pebbles beneath the moon.
Mice in shoes tap across the path,
Revelry sparkles like a bath.

Hidden glee in every nook,
Squirrels dosed with a storybook.
Branches shake with laughter's sound,
As the forest spins joy around.

Frogs in fancy coats leap about,
With every croak, they laugh and shout.
Nature's jesters, in playful spree,
Invite us all to join with glee.

Grins in the Gnarled Knots

Among the knots where secrets sleep,
Lies a jest made for laughter's keep.
A raccoon with a twinkling eye,
Shares a joke with a blushing sky.

Old gnarled trees wear their smiles bright,
Casting shadows in the fading light.
Mushrooms dance in their silly shoes,
Catching whispers of the woodsy blues.

With every twist, the branches play,
Hiding giggles in the earthen clay.
A woodpecker taps with cheeky flair,
As if to say, 'Come join me there!'

In the glade where the wild things roam,
We find the laughter that feels like home.
A hearty chuckle in nature's plot,
Brings joy to the gnarled, happy spot.

Happiness Hidden in the Hollow

In the hollow, chuckles bloom,
Echoing softly, dispelling gloom.
A bear with a cap and a grin so wide,
Invites all critters to dance and slide.

Owls in spectacles share their wit,
Crafty tales, they never quit.
Beneath the ferns, giggles take flight,
As twilight wraps the world in light.

The cheerful breeze tells jokes untold,
Spinning tales of brave and bold.
With every rustle, the laughter spreads,
Among the flowers, where whimsy treads.

So come, my friend, to the hollow's glee,
Where mischief thrives, so wild and free.
In nature's embrace, with laughter's sound,
Happiness awaits to astound.

Shadows of Sweetness

In a grove where laughter spills,
Candy whispers around the frills.
Squirrels dance with glee and cheer,
While hidden treats draw all quite near.

Branches creak with sweet delight,
Chasing each other, what a sight!
Nuts and joy in every nook,
Underneath the leafy book.

Beneath the shade, we play and tease,
Ants carry crumbs with natural ease.
Giggles echo, like a breeze,
While nature shares its little keys.

A pop of color, a splash of fun,
In every twig, a chance to run.
With every step, a chuckle bright,
In this sweet world, all feels right.

Giggles Among the Branches

Up in the trees, mischief brews,
With laughter soft as morning dew.
Leaves chuckle as they sway and wriggle,
Squirrels leap, their tails a giggle.

Beneath the boughs, a game unfolds,
Secrets shared, or so we're told.
Each rustling leaf, a playful wink,
In this realm where sweets all link.

Pinecones drop with playful clatter,
A chorus of laughter, what's the matter?
Nature smiles, inviting the fun,
While shadows dance and sunlight runs.

Secrets of the Swaying Trees

Whispers float through leafy dreams,
As pranks thrive in playful schemes.
Buds break open, laughter swells,
In secret spots where joy compels.

Twigs entwine like gossip sweet,
While giggles hide near roots and feet.
The breeze carries tales from above,
Between the limbs, we find our love.

Mirthful squirrels and jumping jays,
Swinging low in sunny rays.
A treasure trove of light and cheer,
In this green domain, we hold dear.

Echoes of Joy in the Grove

In a circle round the ancient bark,
Laughter blooms where daylight's spark.
Footprints lead to a merry throng,
Where secrets hum a cheerful song.

Cherries blush amidst the green,
A merry dance, a playful scene.
Every branch a story speaks,
As giggles rise, the fun peaks.

The air is thick with joy and jest,
In every nook, a sunny quest.
With every pluck from trees so fair,
Sweet surprises linger in the air.

Chortles in the Glade

In the shade where laughter grows,
Squirrels gather in silly shows.
A jester's hat atop a tree,
Who knew woodlands could be so free?

Breezes tickle, leaves do dance,
Critters join in, taking a chance.
With each rustle, giggles spread,
Joyful echoes, laughter wed.

Carefree Hearts Beneath the Branches

Under branches, friends convene,
The sun peeks through, a golden sheen.
Tickling toes in blades of grass,
Innocent giggles, let's make it last.

Who dropped the pie? Oh, what a sight!
Creamy laughter takes to flight.
A game of chase around a stump,
In this forest, happiness jumps.

Amusement Among the Abranches

Here amongst the tangled limbs,
Laughter rises, joy just brims.
A raccoon plays with shades of light,
Silly antics that feel just right.

Whispers of whimsy swirl about,
Echoes of chuckles, never a doubt.
A squirrel's leap, a startled scamper,
Life's a stage, we're all the tamper.

Revelry in the Roots

Deep in the roots, where mischief brews,
A patch of daisies in playful hues.
Froggies croak in rhythmic rolls,
While giggling elves dance with souls.

Beneath the boughs where shadows blend,
Chasing whispers, our laughs extend.
In this realm of jolly tricks,
Nature crafts its clever flicks.

Mischief in the Twisting Boughs

In the branches high, a plan unfolds,
Squirrels plotting mischief, brave and bold.
With acorns flying through the air,
Laughter echoing everywhere.

Leaves are rustling, secrets shared,
While chipmunks dance, completely unprepared.
A game of chase, they zip and zoom,
Creating chaos in the leafy room.

Birds join in, chirping with glee,
As they watch the show from their lofty tree.
A tumble and a roll, what a sight!
Nature's jesters, pure delight.

As twilight falls, shadows grow long,
In the merry grove, all sing along.
For mischief thrives where laughter's found,
In twisting boughs, happiness abound.

Glee Wrapped in Green

Amidst the foliage, smiles take flight,
Joyful whispers beneath the bright light.
Grass tickles toes, a playful scene,
With sunbeams dancing in vibrant green.

The bushes giggle, leaves sway low,
Creating shadows that twinkle and glow.
A wild game of hide and seek,
With laughter echoing, never bleak.

Butterflies flit with a vibrant swirl,
In this haven where joy can unfurl.
A treasure hunt led by the breeze,
Uncovering wonders with youthful ease.

Under this canopy, bliss is found,
As glee wraps around, sweet and sound.
The magic of nature, simple and free,
A tapestry woven in harmony.

Giggles Under the Arbor

Under the arbor, spirits play,
Joyful giggles fill the day.
Children chase the dappled light,
Creating laughter that feels just right.

A game of tag among the vines,
Where every corner holds surprise designs.
The breeze carries tales we dare to spin,
As smiles stretch wide, and laughter begins.

Their antics weave a playful spell,
Echoing stories only trees can tell.
With petals tossed in the fragrant air,
Every moment is a breath of flair.

So gather close, let worries cease,
In this wonderland, discover peace.
For joy is lurking, just take a peek,
In giggles shared, the heart grows sleek.

Playful Shadows in the Glade

In the glade where shadows waltz,
Whispers of laughter blossom like a vault.
With mischief dancing between the trees,
Joyful echoes float on the breeze.

Frolicking feet leave their trace,
As laughter twirls with the light's embrace.
A handmade crown from the wildflowers,
Turns every hour into magic powers.

Crickets chirp a rhythmic song,
In this haven where we belong.
Fireflies glow, a twinkling crew,
Adding sparkle to the evening's hue.

Underneath the watchful skies,
Every shadow holds a surprise.
With playful hearts and dreams alight,
In the glade, we find delight.

Humor in the Hollow

In the hollow, giggles sprout,
Squirrels wear hats, and dance about.
A raccoon with a spoon, oh what a sight,
Baking pies by the moonlight.

The owls gossip in silly tones,
While frogs play checkers on old stones.
A jester crow hops on a log,
Cracking jokes at the back of the fog.

Trees wiggle their branches in delight,
As the stars wink in the night.
Nature's laughter fills the air,
With tickles and quirks everywhere.

In this hollow, joy never stops,
Lizards wear ties and do funny flops.
A concert of chuckles all around,
In the heart of the woods, humor's found.

Joyous Jive in the Jungle

In the jungle, laughter roars,
Giraffes wear shoes and dance on floors.
Monkeys juggle with bright bananas,
While parrots throw in goofy drama.

The elephants stomp a jolly beat,
Twirling gracefully on their feet.
A sloth in a tutu joins the fun,
Swinging slowly under the sun.

Crocodiles crack jokes, oh what a scene,
While frogs make symphonies—what a team!
The lions laugh, not one bit fierce,
Trading puns as the day they pierce.

Joy hands out giggles in this place,
Every creature wears a joyful face.
In this jungle, it's a grand parade,
Where the breeze carries laughter, unafraid.

Sunny Smirks Beneath the Sun

Beneath the sun, a quirky scene,
Worms wear glasses, keeping it keen.
The daisies droop, but smile wide,
As the butterflies giggle in pride.

A rabbit tells tales, weaving them bright,
Of adventures that stretch through the night.
With carrots in hand, they all lean in,
To hear of mischief and where it's been.

Bumblebees buzz a comedic tune,
Tickling petals, making them swoon.
A snail shares puns that make one cheer,
In this sunny realm, nothing to fear.

With every ray and every giggle,
The flowers sway and then we wiggle.
Beneath the sun, life's a fun run,
Joking along, we all come undone.

Radiant Riddles within the Bark

In the park, trees whisper delight,
Telling tales in the soft moonlight.
Riddles echoed from branch to root,
Mysteries solved by a red-toothed brute.

A beetle boasts of his shiny shell,
Claiming he's dined with a wise old owl.
While chipmunks tell tales with a twist,
Of trees that dance and squirrels that missed.

Under the bark, laughter thrums low,
A circle of critters puts on a show.
With giggles and glee, the shadows applaud,
As the moon grins wide, it's perfectly flawed.

Silly words float through the night,
In this vibrant woodland, everything's right.
Radiant riddles spark joy anew,
In the heart of nature, laughter grew.

Hidden Laughter of the Wind

Whispers tickle branches high,
The breeze plays tricks as it floats by.
Leaves giggle as they sway around,
Nature's jesters; laughter is found.

Rustling secrets in the air,
Squirrels dance without a care.
Jokes are carried on the breeze,
Every tree shows how to tease.

Clouds drift by with silly grins,
Dancing shadows lead the spins.
Laughter bounces off the trunk,
In this forest, joy's unshrunk.

Each gust brings a playful cheer,
Nature's circus is quite near.
Listen close, don't miss the fun,
In every rustle, joy has spun.

Chirps of Joy Within the Canopy

Little birds in feathery coats,
Sing their songs, oh how they gloat!
Chirps of laughter fill the air,
Chasing shadows everywhere.

Branches shake with such delight,
Creatures frolic day and night.
Pocketfuls of sunshine bright,
In this canopy, all feels right.

A rabbit hops with playful grace,
Joining in on the merry race.
Every critter plays their part,
In this symphony of heart.

Amid the leaves, secrets soar,
Joy unchecked, forever more.
The whispers, chirps, and gentle sighs,
Bring out laughter from the skies.

Whimsy Among the Wisps

Moonlight dances on the leaves,
Winking spirits play and tease.
Fireflies laugh, they come alive,
In their glow, all dreams can thrive.

The owls hoot in rhythmic beats,
As branches sway to secret treats.
Soft sighs fill the night so clear,
Nature's beauty draws us near.

Mischief blooms where shadows play,
Every nook holds joy at bay.
Childlike giggles even flow,
In the twilight's gentle glow.

Raccoons stumble, clumsy and bold,
Their sly tricks never get old.
In this realm, the night is fun,
Where every whimsy has begun.

Silliness in the Solstice

Beneath the sun's bright, vibrant dance,
Flowers sway, caught in a trance.
Bees buzz by with cheeky grins,
In every petal, joy begins.

Jumping crickets, laugh aloud,
Their chorus swells, so proud, so loud.
Dandelions turn to wish,
With every puff, a silly wish.

The sun slips low, and shadows stretch,
Tickling toes, as laughter's fetched.
In this season, we all play,
With sunlight leading the way.

Joyful moments fill the day,
Nature's laughter come what may.
In every corner, fun's in bloom,
The solstice brings us all to zoom.

Smirks in the Swaying Sprigs

Beneath the branches, giggles rise,
A squirrel steals snacks, oh what a surprise!
With acorns in hand, they dance in glee,
Nature's jesters, wild and free.

Leaves whisper secrets, rustles abound,
A raccoon winks, then tumbles down.
Laughter erupts from the mossy ground,
In this green circus, joy is found.

Sunlight twinkles, shadows play,
A chipmunk prances, brightening the day.
With every twist, a new joke's spun,
In the sway of sprigs, we all have fun.

Nature's comedy, no script in sight,
In this leafy stage, everything's light.
With each little poke and teasing grin,
The world feels brighter, let the fun begin.

Cheer from the Canopied Haven

Under the archway, laughter rings,
Birds chirp tunes with wobbly wings.
A fox does a jig, just for delight,
As sunlight dances, oh what a sight!

Branches sway like they're in a trance,
Nature's own stage for a clumsy dance.
With every leap, a playful thud,
Joy spills like water, bubbling flood.

There's mischief lurking beneath the leaves,
A playful breeze that teases and weaves.
With every chuckle, the heart takes flight,
In this canopied world, everything's bright.

Clouds float by, soft as cream,
Frolicking friends in a daydream.
With giggles shared, we all belong,
In this haven, we sing our song.

Buoyant Hearts Among the Trees

Swinging high on branches bold,
Childlike joy that never grows old.
Lemonade stands, a sticky affair,
With every sip, laughter fills the air.

Dancing shadows on the ground,
A playful breeze whirls all around.
A critter hops, a playful tease,
In this realm, we are at ease.

Little feet scamper, races begin,
Who can run fastest, who'll win?
In this game of giggles and spry,
Buoyant hearts soar, reaching the sky.

Sunset paints the skies with glee,
Painting tales from every tree.
With every chuckle, freedom's found,
Among the trees where joy abounds.

Mirthful Moments in the Meadow

Butterflies flutter, a colorful dance,
While daisies sway in a joyous trance.
Each step a jig on the grassy stage,
As laughter leans into every age.

Buzzy bees hum their silly tune,
A kitten rolls under the warm afternoon.
With every twist of playful fate,
The meadow chuckles, never late.

Picnic spreads with treats galore,
As crumbs fly 'round, they beg for more.
Tails wagging, a dog leaps high,
While friends share stories under the sky.

With every moment, joy drips sweet,
In this funny paradise, we feel complete.
With smiles exchanged and laughter shared,
In the meadow's embrace, we are ensnared.

Frothy Laughter of Leaves

In the trees, a giggle sways,
Rustling limbs in sunny rays.
Squirrels dance on branches high,
Chasing shadows as they fly.

Whispers float in gentle breeze,
Cheeky jokes shared with the trees.
Barking dogs and chattering birds,
The forest sings, it strains the words.

Twigs are bent with playful jest,
Nature's glee put to the test.
Every rustle, every cheer,
Seems to tickle every ear.

Amidst the boughs where laughter grows,
A symphony of joy bestows.
Giggles tumble, leaves take flight,
In the woods, all feels just right.

Grins in the Green

Underneath a leafy dome,
Nature crafts a laughing home.
Bright-eyed critters play in sight,
Chasing giggles, pure delight.

Beneath the blooms, a friendly tease,
Flowers chuckle in the breeze.
Colors splash like paint on floor,
Every hue shouts, 'Give us more!'

Rabbits hop with silly grace,
Wobbling tails in a race.
Even the rocks share a smile,
Joking softly all the while.

Sunbeams wink through leafy veil,
Casting shadows, a playful trail.
In this realm where laughter spills,
Every moment brings sweet thrills.

Radiance Amidst the Twigs

Up above, the sunbeam grins,
Shining bright where joy begins.
Crickets chirp their merry tunes,
Dancing light beneath the moons.

Branches sway with laughter's call,
Nature's jest, a joyful sprawl.
Swaying vines twist and twirl,
Lazy leaves in a lazy whirl.

Whimsical winds tell tales so sly,
As clouds drift like a soft lullaby.
Every rustle, a jest afloat,
In this realm, joy is the quote.

Mirthful whispers paint the air,
In this space, no shade of care.
Radiance glows where giggles grow,
Every nook, a fancy show.

Forest Frolics

Beneath the trees, the mischief blooms,
Where laughter bounces on soft plumes.
Buddies gather, spirits pirouette,
In a world where joy is set.

Lively sprites flit through the glade,
With every leap, new pranks are made.
Eager whispers paint the air,
In this glorious wonder, so rare.

Mushrooms caper, fungi cheer,
Embracing giggles far and near.
Brighty-eyed, the critters cheer,
Frolics weave through every sphere.

In the woods where jesters tread,
Every footfall leaves a thread.
With hearts lifted, let's embark,
In the forest, light and spark.

Breezy Banter Beneath the Boughs

Under branches wide and green,
Laughter dances, light and keen.
Squirrels chatter, plotting schemes,
Jokes are woven in sunbeam dreams.

A breeze tickles, leaves all sway,
Funny faces at play each day.
The bark might chuckle if it could,
Nature's comedy feels so good.

Branches wave like playful hands,
Whispers travel across the lands.
With every giggle, spirits soar,
Underneath, we crave for more.

The shade provides a stage for glee,
Come join the fun, you'll see!
Each rustle holds a silly tale,
Where laughter thrives and woes grow pale.

Revels in the Rustling

Amidst the leaves, a giggle stirs,
Rustling sounds play games of furs.
The wind calls out with cheeky flair,
Tickling trees in their leafy hair.

Branches bend with laughter bold,
Whispering secrets, stories told.
Under canopies, jesters leap,
In shadowy hideaways, we peep.

Frolicsome breezes join the fun,
Every leaf becomes a pun.
The sun, a spotlight up above,
Casting shadows full of love.

So gather round, the laughter flows,
Every rustle, a joke that grows.
In the rustling, joy does gleam,
Nature's laughter, a cherished dream.

Cheer from Above

From above, the branches sway,
Cheerful chirps bright up the day.
Birds compose their silly songs,
With feathery fun that lasts so long.

Clouds drift by with goofy grins,
As sunlight spills, the laughter begins.
Tickled leaves giggle in replies,
Waving hands of green, oh my!

A playful wind swirls 'round the tree,
Carrying mirth, wild and free.
Each whispered joke stirs giggles near,
Echoing joy for all to hear.

Up above, the world's a stage,
Where every critter shares a page.
With cheerful antics up so high,
Nature's laughter fills the sky!

Fantasies in the Foliage

In leafy realms, where dreams take flight,
Fantasies bloom in dappled light.
Mice in top hats dance around,
While shadows prance upon the ground.

The trees conspire with playful glee,
Turning whispers into a spree.
Reading stories of fun and flair,
In the leaves, we find our care.

Fairies tickle the sleeping blooms,
Rustling softly in secret rooms.
Every sigh of the grass around,
Is like a laugh that knows no bounds.

So wander here where whimsy glows,
Amidst the twirls of light and prose.
In the foliage, let laughter reign,
Crafting dreams on joy's sweet train.

Smiles beneath the Old Oak

Beneath the branches, shadows play,
Laughter echoes, brightens the day.
Squirrels dance with nuts in tow,
Join their antics, let joy flow.

Children giggle, rolling free,
Tickling grass, a sight to see.
The old oak whispers soft and low,
Tales of humor from long ago.

Birds in chorus, chirpy delight,
Chasing sunbeams, taking flight.
Nature's comedy, wild and bold,
A giggle fest, a sight to behold.

Laughter swirls like autumn leaves,
In this haven, joy never leaves.
Beneath the oak, where smiles grow,
We find our heartstrings in a row.

Revelry in the Rustling Foliage

Windswept leaves begin to sway,
Rustling secrets in a playful way.
With every gust, a giggle shared,
Nature's jesters have nothing spared.

A squirrel slips, it takes a fall,
Bounce back quick, let laughter call.
Moments wrapped in leafy green,
Joyful chaos, a lively scene.

Sunlight dapples through the trees,
Tickles the skin, whispers a tease.
Frolicsome breezes brush by,
With a wink, they zip and fly.

In the foliage, spirits rise,
Every rustle, a new surprise.
Nature's party, a wild spree,
Come join the fun, it's the place to be!

Chuckles among the Conifers

Among the pines, a sneaky breeze,
Tickles noses, aiming to please.
Needles fall like jokes on trail,
Giggles burst, it's never stale.

Chipmunks chatter, spinning tales,
Their tiny paws, like tiny sails.
Coniferous hugs, so furry and bright,
Chasing shadows, what a sight!

A playful crow perched on high,
Caws a riddle, oh my, oh my!
With every caw, laughs resonate,
In the company of fun that's great.

Here among needles, joy takes root,
With every chuckle, life's a hoot.
In this forest of humor, we flourish,
Where fun and laughter, we nourish.

Mirth among the Mossy Roots

Mossy carpets beneath our feet,
A giggling patch, where animals meet.
Roots like fingers, tease and tug,
In this realm, we pull and shrug.

An owl drops wisdom, wrapped in jest,
As rabbits hop, put to the test.
Nature's rascals play peek-a-boo,
In this green realm, giggles accrue.

Frogs leap in their froggy dance,
Croaking songs that make us prance.
Under ferns, the laughter slips,
As squirrels share their sneaky tips.

Mirth entwined in roots so thick,
Each chuckle follows like a flick.
Among the moss, it's never rote,
In laughter's cradle, we gloat.

Gleeful Glee in the Grove

In the shade where giggles play,
Frolicsome squirrels dance away.
A breeze whispers jokes, so spry,
While leaves join in with a happy sigh.

Giggling owls make a hoot,
Bouncing bunnies start to scoot.
Sunlight winks through the trees,
Nature's humor floats with ease.

Nature's Softest Laughs

Beneath the boughs, a tickle reigns,
Dancing shadows, playful strains.
A playful breeze with a tickling touch,
Rustles leaves that giggle so much.

The brook chuckles, bubbling with cheer,
While butterflies flutter near and dear.
In this merry, leafy retreat,
Every corner holds a funny beat.

Moments of Merriment Amid the Leaves

Jolly critters in a race,
Chasing shadows, finding grace.
With a pitter-patter, a charming show,
Laughter echoes, soft and low.

Acorns tumble, plop and roll,
Nature's laughter, pure and whole.
Sunshine spills like warm delight,
As branches sway in the soft twilight.

Silly Secrets Among the Saplings

Underneath the leafy veil,
Squirrels plot a grand detail.
Whispers carried on the breeze,
Nature chuckles with such ease.

Twinkling lights and giggling trees,
Marshmallow clouds, a sweet tease.
In the glen where laughter stirs,
Joyful moments in furry fur.

Whispers of Delight in the Dappled Light

In the shade where squirrels play,
Little giggles dance and sway.
Sunbeams tickle leaves so bright,
As laughter echoes, pure delight.

Rustling branches, secrets shared,
Breezy whispers, none compared.
Nature's chuckles fill the air,
With every step, a joyful flare.

Leafy Laughter

Green canopies above our heads,
Tickling toes on nature's beds.
Leaves are giggling all around,
In this place, joy can be found.

Each rustle brings a playful tease,
A melody that floats with ease.
With playful jests from nature's hand,
We chuckle here, a merry band.

Sunny Side Up Under the Sycamores

Eggshell skies and golden rays,
We bask in warmth of sunny days.
With humor sprouting, wild and free,
Under branches, we giggle with glee.

Pancakes flipping, syrup spills,
Joyful mayhem, laughter fills.
In the dappled shade we lay,
Savoring smiles, come what may.

Ephemeral Joys Amidst the Foliage

Moments flit like butterflies,
In the laughter, sweet surprise.
Dancing shadows play a game,
As tickled hearts ignite the flame.

Fleeting whispers, then they fade,
Yet in this joy, we're unafraid.
For each giggle, a little spark,
Lights the wonders, bright and dark.

Joyous Revelations of the Thicket

In the grove where giggles dwell,
A chipmunk slipped on his own shell.
He chased his tail with such great flair,
As woodland creatures paused to stare.

The laughter echoed through the trees,
With antics bright as summer breeze.
A squirrel danced upon a log,
While frogs croaked jokes like silly fog.

A beaver tapped in joyful glee,
Inventing games for all to see.
From vines, the laughter rolled like rain,
A comedy that eased all pain.

Beneath the sky so wide and blue,
The woodland friends all sought their cue.
For in this thicket laughter grows,
And joy, it seems, takes center shows.

Dreamy Laughter in the Dappled Light

In dancing beams of golden glow,
The rabbits put on quite the show.
They spun and tumbled, soft and light,
While shadows giggled at the sight.

Beneath the leaves, on mossy ground,
A secret fest of joy was found.
With acorns tossed and banter sweet,
The day was filled with playful beat.

A wise old owl with eyes so wide,
Said, "Join the fun, don't try to hide!"
He cracked a joke, it took a flight,
And all around rang pure delight.

So join the throng, don't be aloof,
For laughter's song is quite the proof.
In dappled light where dreams convene,
The funny tales are evergreen.

Amusement among the Woodland Spirits

Underneath the grand oak tree,
A gathering of sprites, oh so free!
They popped and twirled in cheerful glee,
Creating antics, quite the spree.

With twinkling eyes and tiny hands,
They played pranks on the forest bands.
A fairy tripped a grumpy toad,
And off they flew down a leafy road.

The hedgehogs rolled in funny hats,
While rabbits laughed at silly spats.
The sound of giggles filled the air,
As spirits danced without a care.

In laughter bright and merry chime,
Nature's jesters stood the test of time.
Among the trees, both wild and free,
The woodland spirits made history!

Enchantment in the Shaded Path

On winding paths where shadows play,
The forest whispers secrets gay.
A curious fox with winks so sly,
Chased after clouds drifting by.

A smiling badger's witty tale,
Had all the blooms begin to flail.
With flowers dancing in the breeze,
And merry giggles from the trees.

The path was lined with splashes bright,
Of mushrooms wearing caps of white.
Each step, a joy, each turn a jest,
Where nature spun her silly quest.

When twilight painted skies in blue,
The forest echoed laughter true.
In shaded paths where joy ignites,
The magic lives in playful sights.

Frolics in the Forest

In the woods where shadows leap,
Squirrels dance, no time for sleep.
Bouncing balls of fur and cheer,
Tickling leaves, they disappear.

A rabbit hops with quite the flair,
Twisting round in joyful air.
Logs and sticks are playthings found,
Echoing laughter all around.

Birds involved in silly pranks,
Making mischief, giving thanks.
Nature chuckles, joins the fun,
Chasing shadows, never done.

Beneath the branches, giggles rise,
Whispers mingle with bright skies.
Woods alive with playful cheer,
Each corner holds a joke to hear.

Glee at Dusk

As twilight falls, the critters play,
Chasing colors as they sway.
Bumbles buzzing through the air,
Share a laugh with the evening fair.

Frogs in ponds, they sing out loud,
Ribbiting jokes to gather a crowd.
Fireflies flash with secret winks,
Lighting up the joy it brings.

Among the trees, a dance unfolds,
A comedy that never grows old.
Laughter weaves through twilight's mist,
An uproarious, moonlit twist.

In this golden hour's grace,
Every shadow wears a face.
Glee at dusk, so sweet and light,
Nature's jesters take to flight.

Jests in the Jangle

In tanglewood, where chaos reigns,
Laughter bubbles, joy remains.
Badger tells a witty tale,
As raccoons join, they laugh and wail.

Branches sway in merry delight,
Creatures frolic, a vibrant sight.
Chirps and laughs, all interspersed,
Every jest is truly rehearsed.

An owl rolls eyes, a wise old sage,
While rabbits prance off every page.
A mischievous fox sets the stage,
With antics that defy the age.

Echoes match the playful song,
Nature's chorus, bright and strong.
Jests in jangle, laughter flows,
In this haven, joy just grows.

Playful Spirits of the Woods

In the woods where spirits gleam,
Hiding games, a lively theme.
Mossy carpets, laughter's ring,
Every heart begins to sing.

A playful breeze, it pulls along,
Leaves that dance, a merry throng.
Chipmunks joke, with peanuts shared,
Creating friendship, love declared.

Beneath the stars, the night is bright,
Frolicking shadows dance in light.
Whispers spread through branches wide,
Nature's jesters, full of pride.

Waves of joy in every breeze,
Laughter echoes through the trees.
Spirits play, their fables weave,
In the woods, we all believe.

Dappled Joys Amidst Nature

In the shade where shadows dance,
A squirrel wears a bright red pants.
He wiggles and he twirls about,
While leaves rustle with a shout.

A bunny hops with such delight,
It seems to dream of flying high.
With every leap, a giggle heard,
A secret joke upon the bird.

The brook babbles with a splash,
While grasshoppers make their dash.
A crow drops by to crack a pun,
It's all just laughter in the sun.

Nature chuckles, soft and clear,
Each critter joined in jolly cheer.
Beneath the trees, it's all a play,
Where joy is found in every sway.

Whimsical Wonders Within the Woodland

In a wood where mushrooms sing,
A fox prances, proud of bling.
With acorns piled atop his head,
He struts around, a king, it's said.

A tiny mouse with cheese so grand,
Wears a hat made from a band.
He leads a dance with grace and flair,
As rabbits twirl, without a care.

The owls hoot jokes, a witty crew,
While fireflies dance in joy anew.
Nature's stage, a laugh parade,
Where every creature's dream is made.

In gnarled roots, a secret lies,
Where giggles rise and never dies.
The woods, a place of charming fun,
A waltz of whimsy, everyone.

Frivolous Frolics in the Forest

Chasing shadows, bright and bold,
A hedgehog spins, a sight to behold.
With tiny feet, he does a jig,
A merry dance, a happy gig.

The trees wear crowns of leafy lace,
While chipmunks play a silly chase.
They tumble down; they roll and laugh,
In nature's book, they write a gaff.

A deer joins in with graceful bounds,
Each hop echoes through the grounds.
Beneath the boughs, a playful breeze,
Tickles the leaves, invites a tease.

With every step, the joy ignites,
The forest sparkles with delights.
In this green realm, the spirit soars,
With every smile, adventure roars.

Touches of Humor Among the Trellis

Twisting vines with tales to tell,
A raccoon plays in hidden well.
He juggles fruits, a merry show,
While crickets chirp, and fireflies glow.

On a fence where sunflowers beam,
A kitten pounces, a silly dream.
She trips on blooms and rolls around,
Amid the laughter, joy is found.

A butterfly in colors bright,
Teases bees with playful flight.
They buzz and giggle, spin and sway,
In this grand garden, all's okay.

At twilight's end, the stars peek through,
Nature's sigh, a joyful view.
With giggles heard, the day departs,
Leaving smiles in tender hearts.

Delight in the Dancing Limbs

Beneath the boughs where shadows play,
 Squirrels scamper, puffed and gay.
They twist and twirl, a jumping spree,
 While whispers laugh in harmony.

A rabbit hops with bopping flair,
 And all the trees just stop and stare.
Their branches sway, a silly show,
 With every leap, the joy will grow.

A breeze joins in, with a cheeky sigh,
 As leaves applaud the antics nigh.
Nature giggles, a gentle tease,
 In this wild world, we all find ease.

What mischief lurks in roots so deep?
 The playful spirits never sleep.
With winks and grins, the forest beams,
 In frolic lands where laughter dreams.

Frolics in the Forest Nook

In secret glades where giggles churn,
The critters dance with no concern.
A fox will prance, a raccoon grin,
Amid the foliage, pure fun begins.

A friendly crow lets out a caw,
As rabbits leap like they just saw
A funny hat or ticklish breeze,
The merry sounds are sure to please.

Beneath the shade, they jive and bounce,
With every hop, they laugh and flounce.
A froggy croaks in rhythm true,
Nature's band, a nutty crew.

In this nook of joy, wild and free,
All creatures share their jubilee.
As sunlight spills and shadows tease,
The forest sings with perfect ease.

Cheerful Chimes from the Treetops

High above, the branches sway,
With cheerful chimes that bright the day.
A woodpecker taps a merry beat,
While squirrels squeak, and dances greet.

The breezy whispers tickle keen,
As daylight paints a playful scene.
A crew of birds in vibrant hues,
Chirp silly songs, carefree and loose.

Amid the leaves, the laughter swells,
As nature weaves its jolly spells.
Each twinkle wink from branches near,
Brings forth a chuckle, loud and clear.

So lift your eyes to skies so vast,
Join in the fun, let worries pass.
For friends abound in leafy tops,
Where joy erupts and never stops.

Winks of Sunlight Through the Leaves

Sunbeams dance on verdant greens,
Winking through, as nature leans.
The shadows skip, the colors blend,
And every critter finds a friend.

A lizard lounges, tail's a sway,
While butterflies flit in disarray.
A chipmunk's blush, a comical sight,
In this warm patch of sheer delight.

As dappled light paints the forest floor,
The giggles echo, want to soar.
Each leaf does clap for fun's parade,
A spectacle of sunshine made.

So gather round for joys untold,
In this wild world, let laughter unfold.
With every wink, a story starts,
A tapestry of fun, in nature's hearts.

www.ingramcontent.com/pod-product-compliance
Lightning Source LLC
Chambersburg PA
CBHW072145200426
43209CB00051B/722